BUZZERS & BELLS

by
Alex Brinded

©2018
Book Life
King's Lynn
Norfolk PE30 4LS

ISBN: 978-1-78637-305-2

Written by:
Alex Brinded

Edited by:
Holly Duhig

Designed by:
Gareth Liddington

A catalogue record for this book
is available from the British Library.

CONTENTS

Page 4   Making Sound

Page 6   Buzzers Buzz

Page 8   Bells Ring

Page 10   Types of Bell

Page 12   Doorbells

Page 14   Telephones

Page 16   Alarm Bells

Page 20   Counting Down

Page 22   Keeping Time

Page 24   Glossary and Index

Words that look like this can be found in the glossary on page 24.

MAKING SOUND

Buzzers and bells all have different sounds. This is because they are usually used to tell us different things. For example, mobile phones sometimes buzz when someone is calling us.

Church bells tell people about church events.

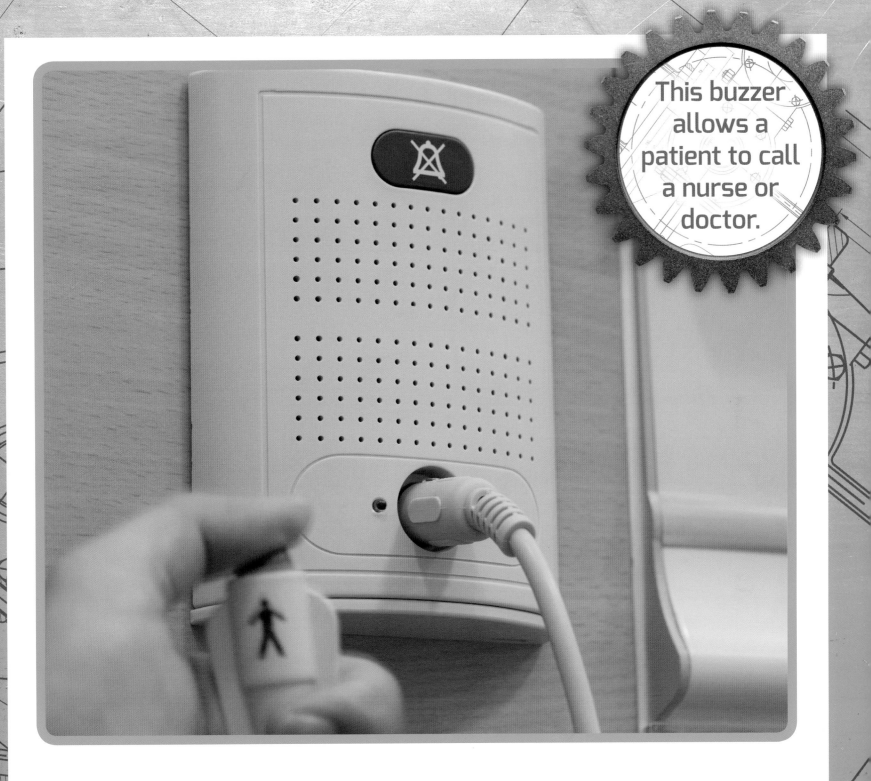

This buzzer allows a patient to call a nurse or doctor.

Electric buzzers and bells are connected to a **circuit**. The buzzer or bell works when electricity flows around the circuit.

BUZZERS BUZZ

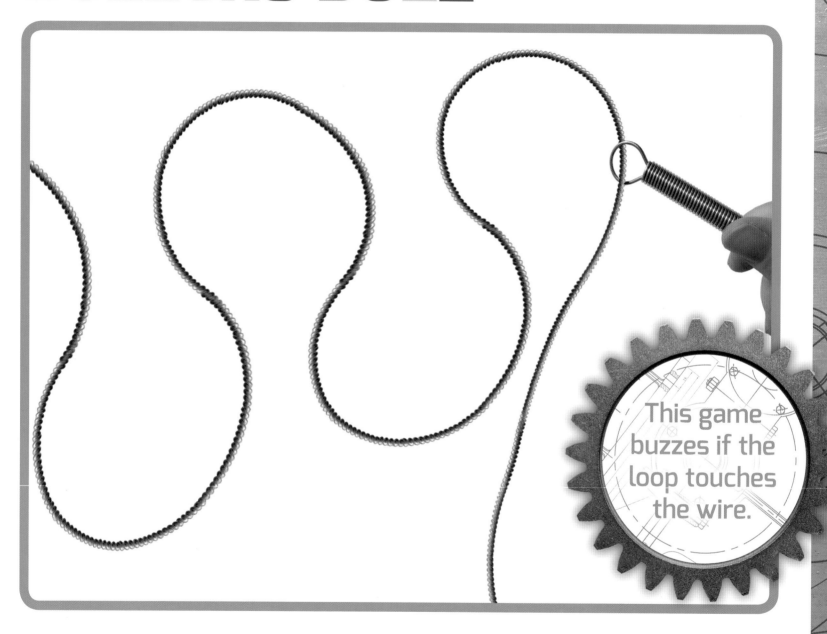

This game buzzes if the loop touches the wire.

Devices that buzz have to be **triggered**. For example, alarm clocks buzz and ring when the clock-hands reach the time that has been set.

Some buzzers have small **motors** which buzz when they spin. The motor will spin a wheel, which may be attached to a weight. When it spins really quickly the whole device shakes.

Electric toothbrushes buzz because of a spinning motor.

BELLS RING

A bell rings when a clapper strikes it. The clapper is like a hammer. It hits the bell and makes it **vibrate**. Bells can have clappers on the inside or on the outside.

Clapper

These clappers are on the inside of these bells.

Bike Bell

Hand Bell

Service Bell

Big Bell

TYPES OF BELL

This clapper is on the outside of the bell.

Some bells are electric and some are **manual**. A bike bell is manual because a cyclist has to press and release a lever for the clapper strike the bell. Bike bells warn other road users there is a cyclist.

In electric bells, electricity makes the clapper hit the bell. The clapper hits the bell again and again while the electricity flows. When the electricity stops the clapper stops too.

School Bell

DOORBELLS

A doorbell is a type of electric bell. When you press the button on a doorbell, electricity flows through the circuit. This electricity causes a clapper to hit a bell.

Doorbells can usually be heard all around the house.

In a block of **flats**, each flat has its own doorbell. The front door for the whole block can be unlocked from inside each flat.

The person at the door will hear a buzzer sound to let them know they can go in.

TELEPHONES

Old telephones had bells on them, which would ring when someone called. The call triggered the clapper. People say "I'll ring you" because telephone bells would ring!

Modern mobile phones buzz when a call or message is received. This buzzing sound is made by a tiny motor turning a weight. The weight is moved very fast which makes the phone shake.

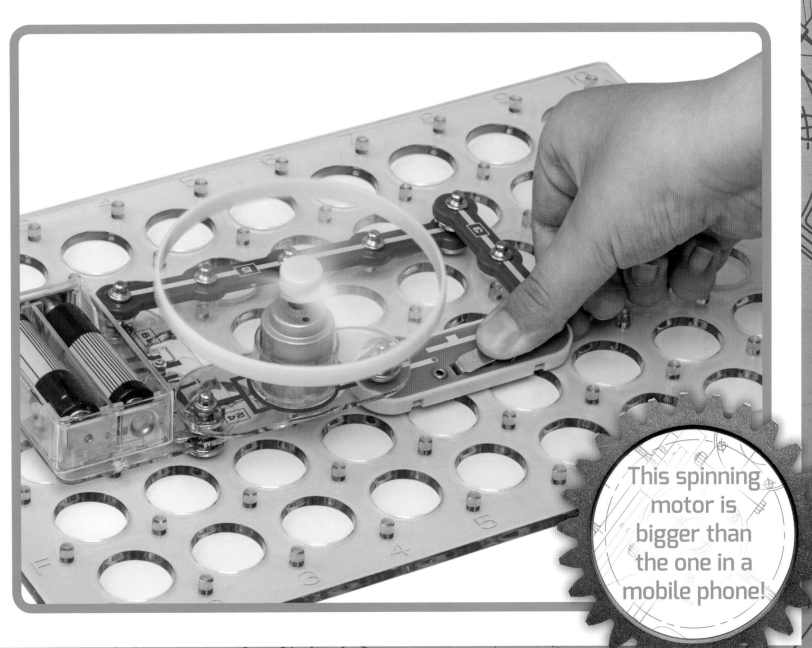

This spinning motor is bigger than the one in a mobile phone!

ALARM BELLS

Fire alarms make a noise when a fire is detected. When a fire alarm sounds everyone must leave the building safely. Fire alarms can be bells, **sirens** or horns.

Fire alarms can be triggered by smoke or heat.

Smoke detectors can be found in schools and homes. If there is smoke in the room, the bell inside the smoke detector makes a loud noise.

The quicker the fire brigade can get to the fire, the easier it will be to put it out.

Emergency services have to get to an emergency as quickly as possible. If they hear the alarm bell at the fire station, they have to move fast to get to the emergency in time.

Old fire engines had bells so vehicles would hear them coming and let them pass. Fire engines, police cars and ambulances now use sirens. Sirens are louder and easier for drivers to hear.

COUNTING DOWN

Timers are clocks that count down and measure time. When they reach zero, an alarm goes off that buzzes or rings to tell you the time is up.

A microwave has a timer that counts down as food or drink is heated. The microwave triggers a bell when the timer reaches zero to tell you that it has finished.

KEEPING TIME

These loudspeakers make the buzzer sound louder.

In sports such as basketball and ice hockey a loud buzzer marks the end of each **period** of play. This buzzer has to be loud enough for players to hear over the noise of the crowd.

A school bell tells students and teachers when classes start and finish. The sound can be heard throughout the school so that everyone can get to their classes on time.

GLOSSARY

circuit	wires that connect electrical devices together
devices	a machines that are made for one thing
flats	homes that are part of a larger building
manual	operated by a person
motors	machines that change electrical energy into movement
period	an amount of time
sirens	very loud warning devices
triggered	set off
vibrate	shaking a lot

INDEX

alarm 6, 16, 18, 20

device 6-7

timer 20

circuit 5, 12

motor 7, 15

vibrate 8

clapper 8, 10-12, 14

phone 4, 14-15

FIRE

↓ PULL DOWN ↓